Daniel Boone
Into the Wilderness

Jennifer Kroll

Consultant
Glenn Manns, M.A.
Ohio Valley Educational Cooperative

Publishing Credits
Rachelle Cracchiolo, M.S.Ed., *Publisher*
Emily R. Smith, M.A.Ed., *VP of Content Development*
Véronique Bos, *Creative Director*
Dona Herweck Rice, *Senior Content Manager*
Robin Erickson, *Art Director*

Image Credits: cover The Granger Collection; p.1 The Granger Collection; p.4 Library of Congress, [LC-USZ62-101385]; p.5 (top) State Historical Society of Missouri, (bottom) Jupiterimages/Getty Images; p.6 Library of Congress, [LC-DIG-pga-02659]; p.7 The Granger Collection; p.8 Jim Parkin/Shutterstock; p.9 Stock Montage/Getty Images; p.10 The Granger Collection; p.11 (top) Alicia Dearmin/Dreamstime, (bottom) Russell Shively/Shutterstock; p.12 Picture History/Newscom; p.13 (top) North Wind Picture Archives, (bottom) Virginia Historical Society; p.14 The Granger Collection; p.15 The Granger Collection; p.16 Library of Congress; p.17 The Granger Collection; p.18 Don Bendickson/Shuttertock; p.19 North Wind Picture Archives; p.20 Keith R. Neely; p.21 Library of Congress, [LC-USZ62-1431]; p.22 State Historical Society of Missouri; p.23 North Wind Picture Archives; p.24-25 State Historical Society of Missouri; p.26 Sharon Day/Shutterstock; p.27 North Wind Picture Archives; p.28 (left) Library of Congress, [LC-DIG-pga-02659], (right) Picture History/Newscom; p.29 (left) The Granger Collection, (right) State Historical Society of Missouri; p.32 (top) tonobalaguerf/Melinda Fawver/Shutterstock, (bottom) Alexey Stiop/Shutterstock

TCM | Teacher Created Materials

5482 Argosy Avenue
Huntington Beach, CA 92649
www.tcmpub.com
ISBN 979-8-7659-0071-0
© 2022 Teacher Created Materials, Inc.

Table of Contents

The Woodsman 4
A Path to Follow 12
Trouble in Kentucky 16
Going West 24
Time Line 28
Glossary 30
Index 31
Americans Today 32

The Woodsman

Daniel Boone was born in 1734 in Pennsylvania (pen-suhl-VAYN-yuh). Daniel loved to be outdoors. He liked to hunt and trap animals in the woods.

This is Daniel's childhood home.

Daniel hunted when he was young.

Fun Fact

Daniel Boone did not like raccoon caps. But many people think he did.

Daniel grew up. He married Rebecca Bryan. They lived in Virginia (ver-JIN-yuh). Daniel and Rebecca had 10 children. Daniel earned money hunting and trapping.

Rebecca holds their sleeping son.

Daniel hunted as an adult too.

7

The Boones lived near mountains. Few **settlers** had crossed the mountains to get to Kentucky (kuhn-TUHK-ee). That was Shawnee (SHAW-nee) Indian hunting land. The Shawnee peoples hunted bison there. Daniel hiked through a **gap** in the mountains.

Fun Fact

Kentucky is a Shawnee word. It means "place of fields."

Daniel looks at the land in Kentucky.

Daniel loved new places. He and some friends hunted in Kentucky. But, they were on Shawnee land. Shawnee Indians stopped the men. They took the men's furs and supplies. The furs were worth money.

Daniel and his friends explore Kentucky.

animal furs

old coins

A Path to Follow

Daniel walked home with empty hands. But he longed to go back to Kentucky. Soon, he did. He was hired to make a road to Kentucky. Others helped him.

Daniel and others clear a road through the **wilderness**.

Fun Fact

Daniel Boone's Wilderness Road was really just a path.

This map shows the path that Daniel cleared.

13

The Boones and other families followed the path. It was called Wilderness Road. They built houses and a **fort** in Kentucky. They named the new place Boonesborough (BOONZ-bur-oh).

Daniel leads settlers along Wilderness Road.

Fort Boonesborough

Trouble in Kentucky

Life in Kentucky was hard. There were disagreements over the land. One day, Daniel's daughter Jemima was on a boat with friends. A few Shawnee men stopped the boat. They took the girls back to their camp.

Fun Fact

Shawnee camps had **wigwams** made of wood and bark.

Some Shawnee men take Jemima and her friends.

The girls could not get away. But they were smart. They were noisy, and they left heel marks as they walked. Daniel and others **tracked** the girls for two days.

Muddy footprints helped Daniel track the girls.

Tecumseh (tih-KUHM-suh) was a well-known Shawnee chief.

Jemima said her father would come. She was right. Daniel found the Shawnee camp. He came crawling through the grass. He took the girls safely away.

Fun Fact

Jemima said the Shawnee peoples were kind to her.

Daniel crawls through the grass.

Daniel's life is honored today with many statues.

Later, Shawnee men stopped Daniel. He needed to show them he was a friend. He agreed to live with them. He stayed with them for five months. Then he ran away.

Shawnee men paint Daniel's face.

Shawnee peoples have a ceremony.

23

Going West

In 1799, Daniel and Rebecca moved west again. They went to Missouri (mi-ZOOR-ee). They lived there for many years. From there, Daniel took trips farther west.

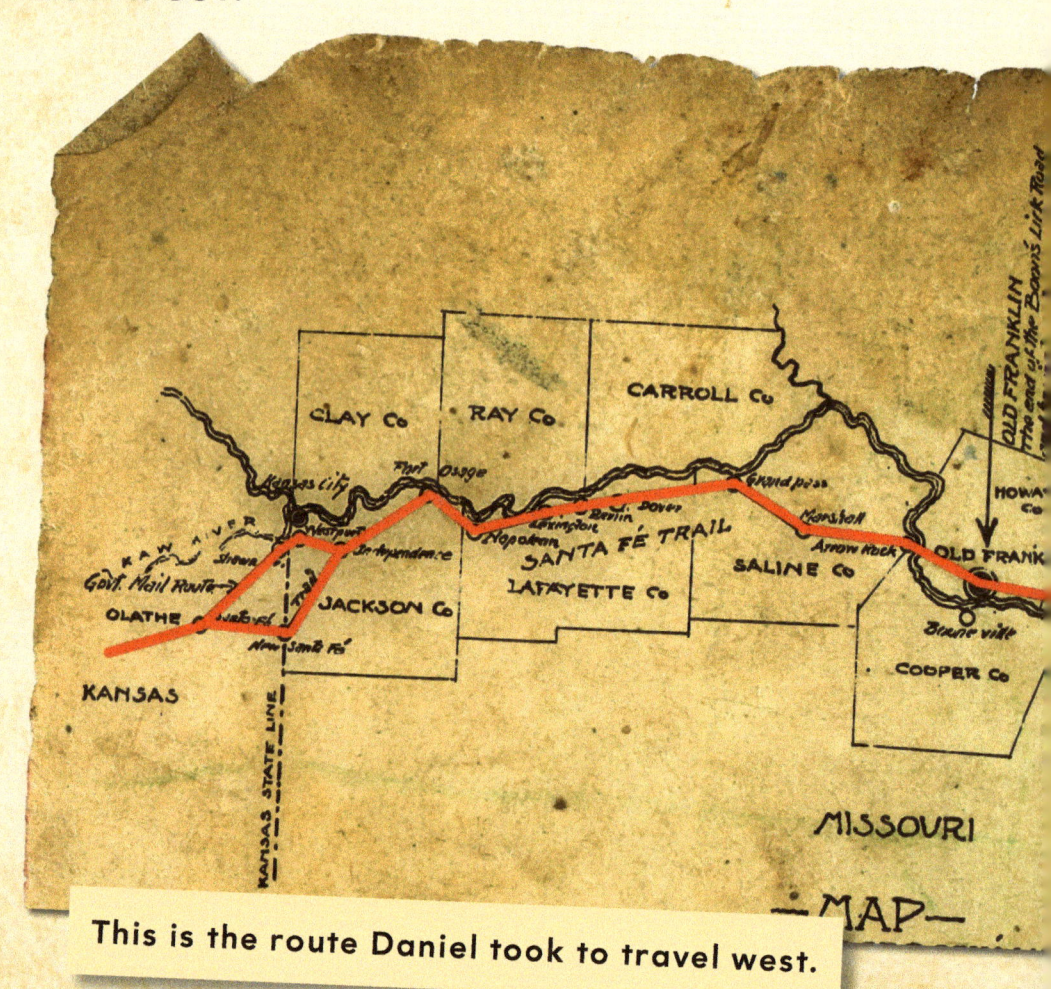

This is the route Daniel took to travel west.

Fun Fact

Daniel walked as far away as Florida and Colorado!

Daniel wanted to see everything. He went all the way to the Rocky Mountains. Daniel felt at home in the wilderness. He had a long, rich life. His adventure finally came to an end when he died in 1820.

Rocky Mountains

Daniel Boone

Time

1734
Daniel Boone is born in Pennsylvania.

1756
Daniel marries Rebecca Bryan.

1775
Daniel helps make Wilderness Road to Kentucky.

Line

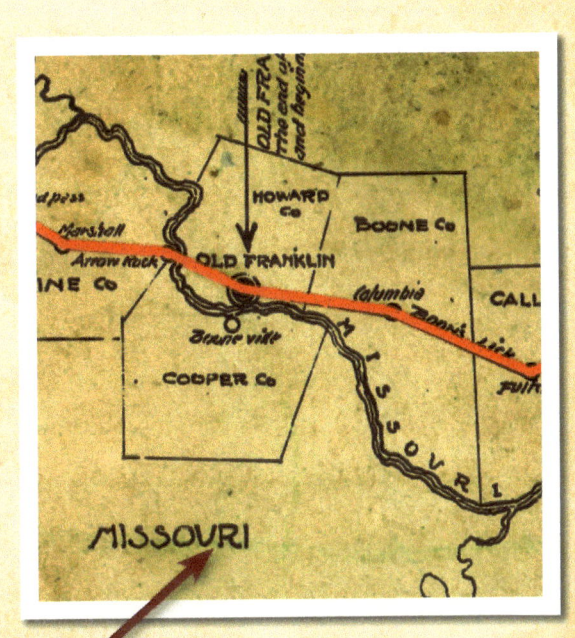

1776
Jemima Boone and her friends are taken by some Shawnee men.

1799
The Boones move to Missouri.

1820
Daniel dies at the age of 85.

Glossary

fort—a strong building used by soldiers to protect an important place

gap—a space between two things or two parts of something

settlers—people who go to live in a new place

tracked—searched for someone or something by following clues until they are found

trap—to catch an animal

wigwams—American Indian huts made using poles and bark

wilderness—a large area of land that has not been changed by people

Index

Boone, Jemima, 16–17, 18, 20, 29

Boone, Rebecca Bryan, 6, 24, 28

Colorado, 25

Florida, 25

Fort Boonesborough, 14–15

Kentucky, 8–10, 12–16, 28

Missouri, 24–25, 29

Pennsylvania, 4, 28

Rocky Mountains, 26

Shawnee peoples, 8, 10, 16–17, 19–20, 22–23, 29

Tecumseh, 19

Virginia, 6

Wilderness Road, 12–14, 28

Americans Today

Today, this family hikes at the Cumberland Gap. Daniel Boone made Wilderness Road through this place. He once hiked in these same woods.